RODEO CLOWN: 12 THINGS TO KNOW

by Samantha S. Bell

STORY LIBRARY
MORE TO EXPLORE

www.12StoryLibrary.com

12-Story Library is an imprint of Bookstaves.

Developed and produced for 12-Story Library by Focus Strategic Communications Inc.

Library of Congress Cataloging-in-Publication Data
Names: Bell, Samantha, author.
Title: Rodeo clown : 12 things to know / by Samantha S. Bell.
Description: Mankato, Minnesota : 12-Story Library, 2022. | Series: Daring and dangerous jobs | Includes bibliographical references and index. |
Audience: Ages 10-13 | Audience: Grades 4-6
Identifiers: LCCN 2020015780 (print) | LCCN 2020015781 (ebook) | ISBN 9781632359438 (library binding) | ISBN 9781632359780 (paperback) | ISBN 9781645821083 (pdf)
Subjects: LCSH: Rodeo clowns--Juvenile literature.
Classification: LCC GV1834.5 .B44 2022 (print) | LCC GV1834.5 (ebook) | DDC 791.8/4--dc23
LC record available at https://lccn.loc.gov/2020015780
LC ebook record available at https://lccn.loc.gov/2020015781

Photographs ©: Mac Armstrong/CC2.0, cover, 1; Phillip W. Kirkland/Shutterstock.com, 4; AB Forces News Collection/Alamy, 4; Delmas Lehman/Shutterstock.com, 5; Keystone Press/Alamy, 5; david hancock/Alamy, 6; SantaMariaTimes/YouTube.com, 7; Gerrit de Heus/Alamy, 7; ZUMA Press, Inc./Alamy, 8; Diane Garcia/Shutterstock.com, 9; ZUMA Press, Inc./Alamy, 9; Matt Cohen/Southcreek Global/ZUMAPRESS.com/Alamy, 10; Shawn Hine/Shutterstock.com, 10; Mette Holm/Alamy, 11; PRCA ProRodeo/YouTube.com, 11; ZUMA Press, Inc./Alamy, 12; Blackfox Images/Alamy, 12; H. Mark Weidman Photography/Alamy, 13; ZUMA Press, Inc./Alamy, 13; H Dillon/Shutterstock.com, 14; Gunter Marx/Alamy, 14; Edward A. Ornelas/ZUMA Press, Inc./Alamy, 15; James Schwabel/Alamy, 15; The Canadian Press/YouTube.com, 16; Yaacov Dagan/Alamy, 17; The Fresno Bee/ZUMA Press/Alamy, 17; T Photography/Shutterstock.com, 18; Stan Rohrer/Alamy, 19; Vanessa van Rensburg/Shutterstock.com, 19; Luc Novovitch/Alamy, 20; Scott Goodno/Alamy, 20; Matt Cohen/Southcreek Global/ZUMAPRESS.com/Alamy, 21; Michelle Gilders/Alamy, 21; James Schwabel/Alamy, 22; Jim Lambert/Alamy, 22; Luc Novovitch/Alamy, 23; Aaron M. Sprecher/UPI/Alamy, 23; CBP Sourced/Alamy, 24; L.E. Baskow/ZUMAPRESS.com/Alamy, 24; Matt Gdowski/Southcreek Global/ZUMAPRESS.com/Alamy, 25; Hemis/Alamy, 26; ZUMA Press, Inc./Alamy, 26; Pat Bonish/Alamy, 27; Cowboy Channel/YouTube.com, 27; Daniel Borzynski/Alamy, 28; Horizons WWP/Alamy, 29; Karl Allen Lugmayer/Alamy, 29

About the Cover

A rodeo clown entertains by riding his horse facing backwards.

Access free, up-to-date content on this topic plus a full digital version of this book. Scan the QR code on page 31 or use your school's login at 12StoryLibrary.com.

Table of Contents

1

Rodeo Clowns Entertain and Protect

Rodeo clowns have unique makeup and outfits.

Some rodeo clowns are called *barrelmen*. They entertain the crowds during the rodeo. But they also help keep the bull riders safe.

When bull riders fall off, the bulls try to hurt them. Barrelmen distract the bulls so riders get away safely. They use large metal barrels to protect themselves. The barrels have thick foam pads both inside and outside. They also have a shelf where the barrelmen can curl up and hide.

Rodeo clowns keep the barrel between them and the bull.

When a rider is in trouble, the barrelman climbs into the barrel and gets the bull's attention. Then he ducks inside and braces himself for a hit by the bull. Sometimes the barrelman is injured. But the rider has more time to escape.

1,500

Average weight in pounds (680 kg) of a rodeo bull

- The barrel has no top or bottom.
- This way, the barrelman can run with the barrel.
- Each barrel is made to fit the size of the clown inside.

THE FIRST BARRELMAN

In the 1920s, fierce Brahma bulls were added to the rodeo ring. Rodeo clowns began distracting the bulls, but it was unsafe for them, too. Then a clown named Jasbo Fulkerson tried using a wooden barrel for protection. He reinforced the outside with old car tire casings.

2

Rodeo Clowns Can Take Classes

Huge, raging bulls are dangerous and why clowns need training.

People who want to become rodeo clowns have a lot to learn. But there's not an official school to attend. Instead, they train in other ways.

New rodeo clowns can attend rodeo training clinics. Many are three days long. At the clinics, new clowns learn basic skills. These classes are taught by successful rodeo clowns. Often the new clowns get into the ring with a bull on the first day.

There are also clinics for clowns who are more advanced. Some students

KEEPING EVERYONE SAFE

During training, instructors emphasize a rodeo clown's duty in the ring. Clowns must first protect the rider. Then they must protect their partner. Then they protect themselves. If a bull rider or a partner is in trouble, the clown will put himself between them and the bull.

Media Clown School teaches ways to distract the bulls and to avoid injury.

are even professionals. They work on improving their skills. Clowns can attend a clinic, work for a while, and then attend another one. For many rodeo clowns, the clinics make up their formal education.

$425

Cost for a three-day training course at Sankey Rodeo School

- The school was started in 1975.
- The school sponsors training clinics throughout the US.
- The courses offered include clowning, bullfighting, and bull riding.

3 Rodeo Clowns Spend a Lot of Time on the Road

Painted faces and funny costumes help keep the crowds entertained.

A rodeo clown might perform in 50 to 100 or more rodeos each year. But rodeos last only a few days in one place. Because of this, rodeo clowns must travel a lot. They have to go where the rodeos are.

Rodeo clowns travel the most during the summer. The weather is warmer. Outdoor venues are more available. This means that

Rodeo clowning is sometimes a family enterprise.

organizations can schedule more rodeos during the week. In the fall and winter, rodeos are more limited. Events are held indoors and mostly on weekends.

For many clowns, the traveling means a lot of time away from their families. But some rodeo clowns take their families with them. J. J. Harrison travels with his wife and children in the summer. He even includes them in his act. The children dress up in costumes and join their dad. They entertain the crowds together.

65,000

Distance in miles (105,000 km) rodeo clown Ronald Burton travels every year

- During Burton's first year, no one would hire him.
- His personality, humor, and hard work helped him become successful.
- Now he travels and performs at rodeos about 250 days a year.

4 Bullfighters Are the Athletes of the Rodeo

Some rodeo clowns are also bullfighters. But they don't have capes or fancy outfits. Their job is to help the riders. When the riders get thrown from bulls, they may be too injured or disoriented to escape. Bullfighters move in to distract the bull. This gives the riders a chance to get back on their feet.

The bullfighters get as close as possible to the bull. As the bull twists around to face them, it's unable to charge. The bullfighters try to anticipate where the bull is going next. Still, they

often get run over or caught by a horn.

At larger rodeos, the jobs of bullfighter and clown are two different positions. The bullfighters protect the riders, and the clowns entertain the crowds. But in smaller rodeos, the clowns fill both roles.

1938

Year the first rodeo clown began bullfighting

- The first bullfight took place at Cheyenne, Wyoming.
- A clown jumped out of the stands and danced around a bull to protect a rider.
- Soon clowns were providing both entertainment and protection.

Wick Peth is a legend among rodeo clowns.

SERIOUS BUSINESS

Wick Peth was born in 1930. In the 1960s, he became the first clown to work only as a bullfighter. He wore makeup, but he didn't want to be funny. Riders appreciated his courage and skills.

Rodeo Clowns Come Prepared

To help avoid injury, the clowns wear loose-fitting clothing. It makes it easier for them to move away if the bull hooks them. The baggy clothes also create a sense of motion. The bulls are attracted to movement. The clothing is usually brightly colored. So is the clown makeup. But these are more to entertain the crowds than attract the bulls.

Many rodeo clowns also wear safety gear underneath their

clothes. This includes protective vests that can cover the front, back, and sides. Some also wear pads to protect their knees, shins, and ankles. Bullfighters and some clowns wear special athletic shorts. The shorts have built-in pockets that hold protective pads. Shoes such as football cleats help the clowns grip the ground. This helps them move out of the way quickly. The clowns also bring their other supplies, including their own barrels.

THINK ABOUT IT

What are some things you wear so you don't get hurt?

$350

Cost of some safety vests

- Some safety vests are made of high-impact plastic.
- The vests can be adjusted to fit the clown.
- They are lightweight. That way, they don't slow down the rodeo clowns.

6 Rodeo Clowns Help Each Other

Rodeo clowns help each other in the ring.

When bull riders fall, they can be seriously injured by the bulls. Right away, bullfighters move in to distract the bull. This gives the rider time to escape. But being close to an angry bull puts the bullfighters in a lot of danger. Sometimes they need help, too. When they are in trouble, the barrelman clown steps in.

The barrelman is a clown that uses a large padded barrel. Sometimes they climb inside of it for protection. But sometimes they use it to get the bull away from the bullfighter. The barrelman places the barrel where it can serve as another target. The bull goes after the barrel instead of the bullfighter. Sometimes the bullfighters can get behind the barrel. This way, the barrel provides them with cover from the bull.

70

Time in seconds of a freestyle bullfight

- In freestyle bullfighting, there are no riders. Bullfighters go one on one against a bull.
- Bullfighters try to stay as close as they can to the bull during the fight.
- Barrelmen are ready to help the bullfighters if they need it.

7

Some Rodeo Careers Aren't Planned

Many rodeo clowns grew up around rodeos. But they didn't always plan on being a part of it. Dennis Halstead was a firefighter in Ontario, Canada. Each year, the fire and police departments come together for a rodeo fundraiser. But one year, the rodeo clown cancelled just one week before the event. Halstead had grown up around rodeos. He volunteered to fill in as the clown. Now, Halstead is one of the top five rodeo clowns in Canada.

J. J. Harrison grew up with rodeos, too. In college, he competed on a rodeo team. After he earned his master's

Harrison refused to be a rodeo clown at first.

degree, he became a middle school science teacher. Then in 2005, a rodeo organizer needed a clown for his bull riding event. They asked Harrison to do it. At first, Harrison said no. But he changed his mind, and soon other rodeos began asking for him. Harrison has become one of the highest-earning rodeo clowns in the US.

8

Years J. J. Harrison worked as a middle school teacher

- For a while, Harrison taught during the school year and worked as a clown during the summers.
- But his rodeo schedule became too full.
- In 2008, he became a full-time rodeo clown.

8 Rodeo Clowns Can Make a Lot of Money

Rodeo clowns are paid each time they perform.

Most rodeo clowns are paid by the rodeo's organizer. They agree on a certain amount of money for each performance. The amount they make depends on the size of the rodeo. It also depends on how much experience the clown has.

Rodeo clowns can earn more than bull riders. Bull riders and other rodeo competitors get paid only when they win. But rodeo clowns and bullfighters get paid each time they perform. New rodeo clowns might earn $200 for a performance.

More experienced clowns can make $2,000. The most talented clowns make between $150,000 and $200,000 per year.

Because rodeo clowns work for themselves, they have to find their own job opportunities. They try to get to know other people who work in rodeos. That way, the rodeo organizers may hire them. Many clowns start by working smaller or amateur rodeos.

$300

Cost of a Professional Rodeo Cowboys Association (PRCA) permit

- Rodeo clowns must have a permit from PRCA to work at their events.
- PRCA is the largest and oldest professional rodeo association.
- PRCA sponsors approximately 600 rodeos every year.

9

Rodeo Clowns Entertain the Crowds

Rodeo clowns put on a comedy act during the rodeo. They fill in when there's a break in the action. There's not just one way to perform. Each rodeo clown puts together their own programs. They may have a whole act planned out. They might tell some jokes. They might sing or dance. Sometimes their children are part of the act. Or they may just interact with the audience.

Some clown acts involve animals. Justin Rumford came up with an act where he fought a miniature zebu bull.

Contact with a charging bull can be painful.

Miniature zebus are one of the smallest breeds of cattle. John Harrison started out in rodeos as a trick rider. When he became a rodeo clown, his horse became part of his act. He does spins and tricks while riding. Dusty Tuckness and Andy Burelle try an even more dangerous stunt. They will sometimes do a backflip over a charging bull.

THINK ABOUT IT

What joke would you tell to a rodeo audience?

9

Age of "Joker" Jett Lorang when he began training as a rodeo clown in 2016

- Jett grew up around rodeos.
- He started doing acts with older clowns.
- He became a featured clown when he was 11 years old.

10 Rodeo Clowns Are Often Injured

Rodeo clowns work hard to avoid injury.

Rodeo clowns and bullfighters wear protective gear under their outfits. But they still suffer a lot of injuries on the job. These include cuts and bruises. They also include broken bones, often several at the same time. Sometimes the clowns get concussions. After they recover from their injuries, they get back into the ring to do it again.

Even in a barrel, the clowns aren't completely safe. One clown described the feeling of being hit while inside the barrel. He said it was like being curled up in a clothes dryer, turning the dryer on, and throwing it down some stairs.

A RUSH OF EXCITEMENT

Adrenaline is a substance released in the body when a person feels a strong emotion, such as excitement or fear. It causes the heart to beat faster. It gives the person more energy. When this happens, it's called an adrenaline rush. Some people experience a rush on roller coasters. Rodeo clowns feel a rush when they get into the ring.

142

Number of bones Leon Coffee has broken

- Coffee has been a rodeo clown since the 1970s.
- He started when he was in high school.
- His worst injury was a head injury.

11

Rodeo Clowns Work at PRB Events

Bull riding is popular across the US.

The most popular event at rodeos is bull riding. In 1992, 20 bull riders got together. They wanted to make bull riding a stand-alone sport. They created the Professional Bull Riders (PBR). The bull riders in the PBR compete against each other all season. The events are televised. Now the sport

has a new group of fans. It has quickly become very popular across the US.

Where there are bull riders, there's a rodeo clown to help keep them safe. In 2006, Flint Rasmussen began working as the exclusive rodeo clown for the PBR. Today, he is one of the most famous rodeo clowns in the world. He entertains the crowd during commercial breaks. Instead of using props, he ad libs his programs. The PBR season runs through the fall, winter, and spring. This means that the PBR rodeo clown can spend summer break at home.

$1 million

Prize money for the World Champion bull rider

- More than 600 bull riders compete for the title.
- They come from the US, Australia, Canada, Brazil, and Mexico.
- The winner becomes the PBR World Champion.

THINK ABOUT IT

How do you like to spend your summer break?

12 Rodeo Clowns Have Reunions

Every two or three years, rodeo clowns, barrelmen, and bullfighters from the US and Canada come together for a reunion. Many of them worked during a time when every clown did all three jobs. The reunion is held to honor these performers.

The reunion lasts three days. They are held in different cities

around the US. The clowns come in their makeup and outfits. They talk about the years they entertained the crowds and protected the bull riders. The community also gets involved. Fans can meet and talk with their favorite performers. They can take selfies with them, too.

1974

Year the first Rodeo Clown Reunion was held

- The reunion was organized by Karl Doering. He was a retired rodeo clown and bullfighter.
- It was held in his hometown of Roseburg, Oregon.
- It was a huge success. The whole community came out to honor the rodeo clowns.

HISTORIAN TO THE CLOWNS

Also known as "Mama Clown," Gail Woerner is an author and a historian. She has written several books about rodeos, including one about rodeo clowns. Woerner has been organizing the reunions since 1993. She plans the events for each day of the reunion.

More Daring and Dangerous Jobs

Bull Rider

Bull riders enter rodeo competitions. They climb onto the backs of angry bulls and hang on as long as possible. Once they fall off, bull riders are in danger of becoming seriously injured or even killed. That's where the clowns come in.

Bareback Rider

Bareback riders try to stay on an untrained horse without a saddle. They hang onto a handle attached to a strap that goes around the horse. Because the ride is so difficult, bareback riders suffer more injuries than other rodeo contestants.

Cattle Ranch Worker

Cattle ranch workers face risks from both animals and machines. They may ride horses that are poorly trained. Those who use large machines can be injured by them. Cows get frightened easily. They may kick or fall on the workers. Bulls may attack the workers.

Glossary

ad lib
To give a speech or performance without preparation.

amateur
A person who participates in an activity without being paid.

clinic
A short, intense course to teach particular skills or subjects.

concussion
A type of brain injury caused by a bump or blow to the head.

disoriented
Feeling confused and out of touch after an injury.

exclusive
Something that is limited to just one person or group and excludes others.

high-impact
Able to withstand a hard hit without breaking.

televised
An event or show that is broadcast or shown on television.

trick rider
A person who does acrobatic stunts while riding on a horse.

venue
A place where an event, such as a rodeo, is held.

Read More

Garrison, Hal. *Bull Riding*. New York, NY: Gareth Stevens, 2018.

Gordon, Nick. *Rodeo Clown*. New York: Scholastic Publishing, 2013.

Hamilton, John. *Rodeo Clown*. Minneapolis, MN: ABDO Publishing, 2015.

Lowe, Mifflin, *The True West: Real Stories about Black Cowboys, Women Sharpshooters, Native-American Rodeo Stars, Pioneering Vaqueros, Celebrity Showmen, and Unsung Heroes in the Wild West*. Minneapolis MN: Bushel & Peck Books, 2020.

Index

About the Author

Samantha S. Bell has written more than 125 nonfiction books for children. She also teaches art and creative writing to children and adults. She lives in the Carolinas with her family and too many cats.